Stockholm Syndrome in a Relationship

Liv Jesson

Published by Liv Jesson Press, 2022.

While every precaution has been taken in the preparation of this book, the publisher assumes no responsibility for errors or omissions, or for damages resulting from the use of the information contained herein.

STOCKHOLM SYNDROME IN A RELATIONSHIP

First edition. September 11, 2022.

Copyright © 2022 Liv Jesson.

ISBN: 979-8215007556

Written by Liv Jesson.

Table of Contents

The author/publisher is not offering professional medical advice or services to the reader. This book is not a substitute for seeking professional help. This publication is based on the author's life experiences and takes no liability for any alleged loss or damages arising from the information in this book. No reproduction, scanning, or use of this publication's content is allowed as per the Copyright, Designs and Patents Act 1988.

www.livjesson.com

Polite note: This book is written in British English and uses British English grammar. For example, 'defense' is written 'defence'.

Introduction

I was in an abusive relationship for thirteen years. My late teens to my early thirties were spent in a state of anxiety, heightened panic, uncertainty, and helplessness due to the toxic relationship I was in. During that time, I was cut off from friends and the majority of my family. I was cheated on, lied to, and deceived unrepentantly.

'Why don't you just leave?' was a sentence that spilt out of people's mouths all too often. 'Pack your things and go back to your mother' or 'You'll meet someone who'll treat you right' became phrases I couldn't stomach hearing any longer. I was frustrated by the fact people would suggest (however covertly) that I was the issue - why didn't I leave? I felt instantly defeated by the fact that people never questioned why my partner couldn't treat me right, only why I wouldn't simply leave.

People just didn't get it. Did I know I was being treated abhorrently? *Yes.* Did it hurt like nothing else in the world? *Yes.* Was I actively trying to cling to the relationship and make it work? Also, *yes.*

But abusive relationships aren't black and white. If you've picked up this book and have read to this point, I might be right in thinking you understand that all too well.

People don't understand the complexity of toxic relationships. To the outside, I was willfully choosing to stay with the person who was abusing me. They couldn't comprehend the truth, nor could I tell them what the truth was: I couldn't leave because I loved my abuser. I wasn't physically stuck with them, but mentally and emotionally, I was beholden to them. I was in their jail, but I was often happy just to be there because it meant I was with my abuser. Ironically, and at the time I didn't see it like this, I held the key to my jail cell. I just could not bring myself to acknowledge this, let alone use the key to free myself. The thought of being without my partner was too much to bear.

The abuse I endured was emotional, mental, and occasionally physical. It didn't start this way, though - abusive relationships never do. When I met my would-be abuser, it felt like he was a piece of the puzzle I'd been missing: he filled me with love, adoration, and words of affirmation. He made me feel special. We made each other laugh, we spent an abundance of time together, and we agreed we were soulmates.

This fuzzy feeling lasted around three months before things began to change. The love bombing ended, and the cruelty took over. The warmth of the past few months suddenly dulled, like a rain cloud looming on a sunny day. A colder, more dismissive side to him began to appear. He didn't like me going out or meeting friends. He took a dislike to my family and refused to meet them, eventually getting angry if I spent too long with them. The things I did - or didn't do - seemed to displease him, and he became beyond critical of me.

Initially, I challenged this change in behaviour, and I tried to set boundaries. When he decided that staying out all night and not letting me know his whereabouts was acceptable behaviour, I tried to make him understand how unfair this was to me. This was four months into the relationship, and it was also the first time he physically assaulted me. Still, and as you may know yourself, he managed to twist this event into me provoking him and 'suffocating' him. The whole event was twisted to make me out to be the instigator, the one who stepped out of line. As remarkable as it is to look back on now, this scenario ended up with me being the one to apologise, a theme that would continue throughout the relationship.

From here, the cycle of abuse continued. Stage one was complete: he'd love bombed me with an idealised version of who he was (a fake, made-up version to lure me in). Now the next stage was in full force. I became anxious about the relationship, worried he would break it off at any point. I couldn't please him. I was isolated by this point, and when I went to work, I was visibly withdrawn and not present. This is the state my partner wanted me to be in. He didn't want me to feel safe or content in the relationship, despite me occasionally still getting glimpses of love from him. He needed me in this heightened state so I would desperately claw to get the 'perfect' relationship we had back. Because I'd fallen so deeply into the trap of being love-bombed, I truly believed the person I'd met initially was still there. I would've done anything to get that back.

The feeling of being trauma bonded to your partner is undoubtedly emotionally and physically damaging. You stop eating, you feel full of dread, you can't think straight, and you develop unhealthy coping mechanisms. It's a living nightmare, and one you can't seem to wake up from. However, as hard as it seems, you don't need to feel this way. There is a way out, and you can take me as proof that Stockholm syndrome in a relationship can be overcome.

It takes some education on the subject, a lot of will and determination, and a want to rediscover your self-worth. I must admit it took me years to go from understanding the trauma bond I had to leaving my abuser for good. I left multiple times before eventually reconciling, just because I couldn't handle the heartache of being without him.

According to *Women Against Abuse*, it takes an average of seven attempts before you leave an abusive relationship for good. I think I exceeded that number, but who's counting - the point is, I did eventually leave for good and I have to tell you, it's the best thing I ever did. It wasn't easy, but I got through it, and now I'm writing this book to help people who are enduring the pain of a relationship they just can't leave.

In this book, I'm going to cover exactly what Stockholm syndrome is in your relationship and what it means for you. I'll go over the signs, the reasons for it, and the cycle of abuse that keeps you trapped in a toxic relationship. I'll take this time to note that I'll use the phrases 'Stockholm syndrome' and 'trauma bonded' interchangeably. They are separate phrases that describe the same thing: the deep emotional connection between the abuser and the person they abuse. I'll also discuss the elements of narcissism that drive someone to abuse the person they're romantically involved with, as well as my favourite thing to discuss: ways you can break the trauma bond. I'll also go into a little more detail about my own experience with Stockholm syndrome in my relationship because I know that I was helped so much by reading about others' experiences while I was in the midst of an abusive relationship.

Before I begin, I'd like to tell you that while the road ahead may not be easy, I assure you it'll be worth it. Please know that even if you can't see it right now, there is light at the end of this tunnel.

Stockholm Syndrome And The Symptoms Of Traumatic Bonding

Years ago, I'd never have believed that Stockholm syndrome could ever be linked to a romantic relationship. When I thought of Stockholm syndrome, I thought of cases where people had been abducted and began to develop feelings for their captors. I envisioned the victim kept in an underground bunker, where their kidnapper was their only saviour, the one person to bring them food and water.

The name originates from the 1973 bank robbery in Stockholm, Sweden, by criminal Jan-Erik Olsson. He took four of the bank's employees hostage for six days during his botched attempts at a robbery. He also enlisted the help of his friend Clark Olofsson to help with his plan. The pair spent 24 hours a day with the three women and one man they'd kidnapped in the bank's vault, eventually releasing them on August 28. The thing that people really couldn't get their head's around was the way the hostages acted when they were freed: not one of them would testify against their captors. In fact, they raised money to help them in their defence. The behaviour of the bank's employees helped coin the term 'Stockholm syndrome'. Still, events like this were mostly unheard of. Then, the following year, the Patty Hearst case made headlines.

I'll quickly cover the extreme events of the Hearst case to explain how Stockholm syndrome became a well-known term, and not to use it as a comparison to your situation. While the relationship you have with your partner is different to the one one Patty had with her captors, the feelings she felt towards them likely run parallel to the ones you feel for your abuser, albeit not in the most obvious way.

I remember the case of Patricia Hearst from a documentary I watched years ago. She was already somewhat famous before her kidnapping by the Symbionese Liberation Army (also called the SLA) in 1974. She is the granddaughter of media businessman William Randolph Hearst, so her name was already well known, but she was well and truly thrust into the media spotlight when she was taken hostage by the SLA. Her case was so intriguing that there have been plenty of documentaries and films made about the events that took place, and even more questions were raised as to why Patty acted the way she did throughout her ordeal.

Hearst was kidnapped in Berkeley, California on the morning of February 4, 1974. The 19-year-old was accosted at gunpoint by a gang of men and women who were later discovered to be part of a group of radicals who we'd later learn were called the SLA. At the forefront of the ultra-left-wing party was Donald DeFreeze, a renowned criminal who headed the SLA and guided their attempts to destroy what they referred to as the 'capitalist state' of America. They kidnapped Patty to garner attention for their cause; after all, Hearst's family were rich and powerful, the very demographic the group were against. Their plan worked, and their army was front-page news for the kidnapping.

The SLA made the most of their newfound notoriety and demanded millions of dollars in order to release Patty. In the background, however, there was more to the SLA's plans than met the eye. They were slowly indoctrinating her by abusing her.

Hearst was kept in a closet for her first week, bound and blindfolded. During this time, she was threatened and told she'd be killed. Eventually, she was let out of her small prison for food, although the blindfold remained tightly on her face. While she was given food, she would overhear the political chats going on around her by the SLA.

She subsequently joined in on these discussions, after which the SLA gave her a torch so she could read in her small cell. She was given mostly political material to read. Weeks passed, and eventually, Patty was told the group were considering whether to kill her or let her stay and fight their cause. She was told to think about the latter possibility, which Patty did, as the SLA then gave her another option: to be set free or stay with them. She chose to stay. It was at this moment her blindfold was taken off and she was able to look at her abusers and captors for the first time. She was subsequently taught to use weapons and was allegedly raped by multiple members of the group.

Still, Patty was adamant she was to remain part of the SLA. The group even released a tape where Hearst announced that she had joined the group and had taken a new name, Tania. Hearst's name soon became synonymous with the term Stockholm Syndrome, particularly when she was spotted on CCTV with the group wielding an assault weapon as she took part in an SLA bank robbery. She was seen shouting orders and brandishing the gun while the group stole cash from the bank's vault.

Patty was finally captured by authorities on September 18, 1975. She was charged with a number of crimes, including the bank robbery. At the time she was arrested, it was noted Patty had changed drastically as a person during her time with the SLA. She had lost a significant amount of weight, her IQ had dropped exceptionally, and she struggled to recall her life prior to the kidnapping. She chain-smoked and had night terrors, things she didn't do before her ordeal. It was clear that the SLA had turned Patty into this - she'd gone into survival mode, and that meant pledging allegiance to the very group that threatened her safety if she didn't comply. Still, there was little information available on Stockholm syndrome back then, and the term trauma bonding still hadn't been coined. Subsequently, Hearst was given two years behind bars for the crimes she committed while part of the SLA.

Stockholm syndrome isn't just used to describe hostage situations

The Patty Hearst case goes some way to show just how much another person can control and manipulate you into behaving how they want you to. While that case might seem like an extreme comparison to the trauma bond we feel in an abusive, controlling relationship, the acts and reactions that occur in these situations are incredibly similar to those exhibited in a toxic partnership. In fact, they run parallel.

Just like Stockholm syndrome was a survival strategy for the bank robbery victims and Patty Hearst, it's a survival tactic for those of us in an abusive relationship, too. We utilise this strategy for the very same reasons Hearst did: to increase our chances of survival (i.e., maintaining the relationship in order to try to make it work) and, more crucially, it's a necessary mental tool we adopt to defend ourselves psychologically against the effects of an abusive, toxic relationship.

Just like in a hostage situation, an abusive relationship often has a big power difference. In the hostage scenario, the captors call the shots. They decide what the captive does, when they eat, how much they get to speak. In an abusive relationship, the abuser calls the shots. They get to control their victim, to choose how their life is lived, and how much say they have in the relationship. Different scenarios, same emotional reaction from the victims.

In short, Stockholm syndrome is something victims of abuse develop to help them cope with the trauma they're enduring. This is shown when the victim becomes deeply attached to their abuser. Just as Patty Hearst became trauma bonded to her abusers to ensure she was kept alive, we victims of abuse do it because we feel tied to our partner, we are worried we won't see our children or pets again, we feel we can't support ourselves, we have nowhere else to go, or we feel utterly helpless at being able to break away from the person we love. Simply put, we are clinging on to survive, convinced we can't live without our partner, no matter how badly they treat us. The alternative is just too unbearable to think about.

Stockholm syndrome is a psychological shift we utilise to *just keep going*.

The manifestation of abuse at the hands of the one person we expect to love and cherish us - our partner - offers distinct symptoms. While every person who's endured the invisible shackles of being trauma bonded to someone has a different scenario, their symptoms remain the same. If you're still trying to ascertain whether you're in the clutches of a trauma bond, these symptoms may help you decide.

Symptom #1: You Want to Appease Your Abuser

This is the symptom most people on the outside looking in just can't seem to wrap their heads around. Wanting to pacify the person who's causing you unbearable emotional suffering is a tactic we use in order to try to protect ourselves. We want to keep our abuser happy so they can't find an excuse to treat us so horribly.

While those outside the relationship see someone willfully doing their best to satisfy their partner's wants, the truth is much more complex and heartbreaking. We do what we can, to the detriment of our self-worth and our mental health, to make sure our spouse isn't upset with us. We walk on eggshells, we watch what we say and how we say it, we act how they want us to act and we ensure we don't 'step out of line'. If we do, for whatever arbitrary reason, upset our partner, we are made all too aware of this fact.

The punishment doled out by the abuser differs from relationship to relationship. It could be the silent treatment, it could be verbal abuse, or it could be the threat of the relationship ending. In my case, I did everything I could to appease my abuser, so they wouldn't walk out the door and turn off their phone for days on end. To the outside, it seemed like I should relish these moments - the times when my abuser wouldn't be there for days at a time, so I could breathe a sigh of relief. In reality, and he knew this, I'd be going out of my mind with anxiety. It was events like this that he would use to cheat on me, although I often wouldn't find this out until months, even years, afterwards. I also knew that when he did eventually return home from these benders - that he would insist I pushed him to do - he would often be drunk. Alcohol always caused my abusive ex to become aggressive.

In the days between him walking out and coming home, I'd be a twisted knot of worry and anxiety. I couldn't eat, I barely functioned. I would be in a heightened state of panic, worried simultaneously about what he was getting up to and what it was going to be like when he got back home. I dreaded yet yearned for him to come home, which is a good way to explain how I felt throughout the entirety of the relationship.

To avoid this punishment, I would do everything within my power to make sure I didn't trigger him.

I would avoid social situations and meeting up with friends. I'd make sure the house was tidy when he returned home. I'd turn my phone notifications off for fear of getting a message while he was there. Sure enough, he'd ask who it was from, or sometimes pick my phone up and take a look for himself. I deleted my social media to avoid angering him or making him think I was being unfaithful. The plethora of things I did, I did to ensure my own mental and emotional safety. This is a surefire sign of Stockholm syndrome.

Appeasing your abuser is a form of self-preservation. If we can keep them happy and pacified, we will survive another day. However, there is a flip side to this act of constantly striving to please our abusers: it strengthens their power over us. It reinforces the power dynamic of the relationship. It shows them that they have control over us, and it boosts their grip on our subservience. The pacification tactic we use is a double-edged sword. We need to utilise it in order to maintain calm, keep the peace, and try to enforce some security in the relationship. However, our abuser spots this as a weakness and uses it to their advantage.

Whatever your spouse knows will hurt you, be it staying out until all hours, the silent treatment, being physically abusive, or spreading lies about you, they will use against you if you don't comply with their expectations of you. Still, we keep on trying to keep our partner happy, because we are often rewarded with a false sense of security about the relationship, a reduction in the abuse doled out, and a period of time where we feel a sense of relief.

Symptom #2: Learned Helplessness

As I touched on earlier, many people outside of the relationship will often wonder aloud why you don't 'just leave' or 'get out' of the situation you're in. Speak to someone, we are often advised: *ask for help*. What people don't understand is that this isn't like sitting through a movie you don't like, where you can just turn it off. It's a relationship, with deep feelings and emotions and implications involved. Leaving an abusive relationship is hard; the abuser has us defeated, controlled, and unable to act without fear.

The abuser works to cultivate an environment where they are the puppet master. They do this in a number of ways: invoking fear, mind games, gaslighting, manipulation, isolation and, sometimes, assault. These soul-crushing acts carried out by our spouse repeatedly work to stop us from fleeing the relationship and help fortify the power they have over us. At the same time, they make it so they are our only source of comfort and familiarity. When we are hurt and upset, often by them, the only place we feel we can turn is to our abuser.

If you think back to being at school or studying for an exam, what did you do to learn the things you needed to remember? You listened to the authority figure - your teacher - who repeated them to you. Not only did they repeat their teachings in every class, but they also explained these things as facts. You took what they said as truth because they'd established themselves as an authority figure. Repetition helps cement these facts in your head.

This is also how an abuser works. Not just spousal abuse, either; if a child is repeatedly told they're stupid, sure enough, they're going to take that as truth, eventually. If an employee is repeatedly told they're the weak link in the team by their boss, they're going to bear that title on their shoulders and it'll reflect in their demeanour. If your mother constantly compares you to your 'prettier' sister, then you're going to mentally carry the title of the 'ugly sister' and accept it as the way it is, no matter how much it hurts, simply because you've been made to think it's the truth. A narcissistic abuser works in this exact way. Over time, their cruel words and actions become your truth.

Even the most outgoing, extroverted, or seemingly 'mentally tough' individual is susceptible to abuse. It creeps up hurtfully yet quietly, eventually becoming a part of your identity. A self-assured person can still fall victim to an abuser. The way these people work means nobody is off-limits. Sure, abusers have preferred personality types, but overall, anybody is fair game. They chip and chip away at their victim until they truly believe they are what the abuser tells them: worthless, stupid, ugly, a waste of time, a burden devoid of value. When you feel all of these horrific things are true, the abuser can make you believe you are lucky to be in a relationship with them. This is their magnum opus - what they strive to achieve. You're well and truly broken when you reach this point.

All of this is summed up in the phrase, 'learned helplessness'.

Once you are convinced that you are less than, always wrong, and of little value, the only constant in your life is your abuser. You no longer have control. They are the only thing you have. Despite all of your faults - of which you are led to believe are many - they're still with you. You can't be without them, because they endure your burden and put up with you despite you not offering them what they 'deserve'. You are helpless because you're been taught you are.

While you feel you can't change things for the better for yourself, i.e., leave or be apart from your partner, you do feel that you can work to maintain the one constant you have: your abuser. This goes back to the first symptom of appeasement, where you do everything you can to keep your partner happy. But, this same effort just does not exist for trying to regain your control and self-esteem: those things are simply gone. Instead of trying to claw back the person you were, you believe you're the person your abuser tells you that you are. You're resigned to the notion you're stuck in this situation.

Symptom #3: Inability To Detach From Your Abuser

It's not a case of you simply 'won't' leave the abuser - you truly feel like you can't. The mere thought of being separated from your spouse is crippling. It's as if your oxygen supply is taken away. You struggle to breathe as the heaviness of the thought sits on your chest. Leaving your abuser isn't just undoable because of the control they have over you, but also because you're so attached to them that you cannot be apart from them.

You'd worry about them, you'd panic about the repercussions of leaving them, you'd miss them, you'd be afraid they'd sabotage your attempt at leaving and punish you further. These contradictory feelings are confusing, but one thing is not: your inability to leave them.

Add to the fact that you've built a life with this person. You may have bills, debts, commitments, pets, and even children with this person. For me, whenever the thought of leaving crept into my mind, I would buckle at the idea of having to leave my dog behind. To others, this may have sounded silly; that I would worry about the very person who made my life so full of hurt and anxiety, and that the thought of being without him and our dog stopped me from leaving.

If you can understand this feeling, then the trauma bond is in full effect. This unwillingness to tear yourself from your abuser and reluctance to face the pain of leaving them in order to heal are classic symptoms of trauma bonding.

The idea that if you leave and endure the initial pain of the breakup, that there's then light at the end of the tunnel, just isn't fathomable. Your loyalty resides with your partner, over everything and everyone, even yourself.

Symptom #4: Sympathising With Your Abuser

This is a true, classic telltale sign of Stockholm syndrome in a relationship. No matter what your abuser does, how they treat you, what they say, where they go, how horribly cruel they are to you, you can always find empathy towards them. You sympathise with their plight, you feel sorry for them, you want to help them and pull them out of the sadness and torment. You feel like you understand your abuser and take pity on them. It could be that you feel sorrow about their difficult childhood, their mental health issues, their insecurities - whatever it is, you end up in a position whereby you view your abuser as a victim themselves.

You take this view either because of their past, things they've told you that hurt them, or what you perceive as their 'self-destructive' actions. Sometimes you can even view them as a victim of themselves. You have endless amounts of empathy for your partner, and this evokes a natural response to 'save' or 'fix' this person because you love them. Abusive individuals tend to seek out empathetic, compassionate people. Likewise, empathetic people tend to look for the good in others, and will try to help their spouse, even if they're hurtful and cruel. It's a horrible combination for the empath, since the abuser takes full advantage of their partner's abundance of compassion and endless stream of forgiveness.

Symptom #5: Protecting The Abuser At All Costs

Be it from their peers, your family, their family, or the police, you do everything in your power to prevent your abuser from being exposed for their actions. You lie to save your abuser facing any negative consequences for their treatment of you, and you'll go out of your way to cover up their actions and paint them in a much more flattering light than they deserve. This isn't just to save face either, it's also because you believe that deep down, your abuser does have goodness and compassion in them, and you don't want them to be berated for their bad behaviour when you know it isn't really who they are. Sadly, it truly is who they are.

Of course, you don't see this while you're in the thick of a trauma bond, and your unwavering hope that your spouse will one day rectify their cruel behaviour ensures you protect them no matter what.

On top of this, there's the fear of what would happen to you if you let the world see your abuser's true colours. You know all too well that you're punished for things that aren't your fault or responsibility, and the exposing of your partner would more than likely be 'your fault'. To stop this unjustified blame, along with the unthinkable abuse that would ensue, you make sure that your spouse sees no outside ramifications for the things they do to you. If family or friends try to intervene or protect you, you can begin to feel resentment towards them for putting you in an impossible situation. If the police somehow become involved, you wish they'd disappear and stop interfering.

These symptoms are a manifestation of the never-ending rotation of abuse. I'll discuss this in more depth in the following chapter, but for now, take a moment to consider the symptoms of Stockholm syndrome and think about how they present themselves in your behaviours and thought patterns. Think about the times you've gone out of your way to pacify your partner to avoid a bout of abuse or a verbal assault. The times you've lied on their behalf to avoid people knowing just how vile your abuser has treated you. The pity you may feel for the very person who willingly hurts you. To confront these symptoms is an important part of the eventual breaking of the trauma bond. While I know the easiest thing to do is to bury any acknowledgement of the damage you've endured, you can only suppress it for so long. It's not a pleasant thing to sit and ruminate on, but it can help you pull yourself out of the cycle of abuse.

Understanding The Cycle of Abuse

Abuse is a cycle. It's a continuous loop of repetitive acts and behaviours that is doomed to continue until one person in the relationship ends it for good and goes no contact. That's likely a difficult thing to comprehend if you're stuck in a trauma bond with your partner. The idea of a life without them feels worse than the pain you're enduring while you're with them. But, to be free from the cycle, you need to understand the cycle of toxicity.

If you've read this far, and are resonating with the things I'm talking about and can honestly apply them to your own relationship, then you're much further ahead on the path to healing than a lot of people in a toxic relationship. The fact that you can accept this as your truth means you're willing to confront difficult facts about your partner and the state of your relationship. It also means the next part I'll discuss - the cycle of abuse that keeps you trauma bonded - will hit home.

It can be hard to try to truly rationalise the actions of your spouse. You wouldn't dream of causing them pain or relishing in their suffering. You don't want game playing, manipulation, or any of the toxicity you currently have in your relationship; you want to love and be loved. It should be as simple as that. You have your partner's back and you want them to have yours.

You have so much empathy and care for your other half, but those compassionate feelings are rarely returned. Not genuinely, anyway. This can make wrapping your head around their true intent for you even harder to digest.

Let me cover the four phases of abuse:

Phase 1: Tension Building

Or, as I sometimes refer to it, the 'Walking on Eggshells' phase. It's during this period, which can sometimes last months, but often lasts days or weeks, that you find your anxiety levels are through the roof. Your abuser, for whatever reason, will feel wronged by you. It could be they're feeling neglected, mistrustful, or like you're not meeting their (often unrealistic) expectations. The tension in the air is unbearable. You don't know how to fix it, and you'd do anything to put whatever you've done right. You don't know if you're coming or going, and you're almost frozen with fear. If you make a misstep, you risk further angering your abuser, which will make the situation ten times worse for you.

During this phase, you endure accusations, yelling, belittlement and a whole bunch of gaslighting. Silent treatment can feel just as nerve-wracking, too - that's the power of the control our partner has over us. We are like a sitting duck during this phase, although we're all too aware that the target is on us. One wrong move can trigger an eruption, something we're desperately trying to avoid. We've been through this enough times to know that whatever we do - or don't do - can't ever stop the rising tension. We also know that the next phase is imminent, no matter how much we try to put it off.

We can sense the tension within the relationship increasing as the days go by. We try whatever we can think of to stop our spouse from becoming angry. For example, if the dog is barking 'too loudly', we will do our best to quieten the noise. If dinner is overcooked, we will try to pacify our abuser, offering to remake it or order food in. If they ask us to buy something specific at the store and we return with the wrong thing, we race back to the shop to correct our mistake. We try our hardest, often to our own detriment, to avoid the next stage of abuse. In doing so, we are continuously enduring this anxiety-riddled phase of tension building.

This phase means we are always having our love and faithfulness put into question. We have to guess what our spouse is sulking about, wondering what we've done to make them withdraw from us. Manipulation, gaslighting, and their hurtful mind games are rife at this stage. To top it all off, we are to blame for everything: how our abuser treats us, what we 'make them' do, and we are the reason our partner feels unhappy. They're not shy in letting us know this, which is ironic since they refuse to set us free. Instead, they choose to enjoy the tight grasp of control they hold over us, pulling us closer to them. This irony is sadly lost on us at the time and we can't see past the fog of manipulation and hurt.

But, the tension building stage never lasts forever. Sure enough, Phase 2 is always one 'misstep' away.

Phase 2: The Incident

A.K.A full-blown abuse. The tension went from simmering to boiling to outright explosive. Whatever triggered it, be it a made up scenario by your partner or by them being upset by something you've done to apparently hurt them, you're going to pay for it. This is what we try our best to avoid during the tension phase, but we know all too well that the incident will happen, regardless. Still, we try in vain to avoid this monumental upset each and every time.

The outburst or onslaught of abuse differs from situation to situation. It could be a barrage of verbal abuse, a bout of physical abuse, or sometimes the abuser's weapon of choice is sexual. The incident is an eruption of pure malice and torture towards the victim, but after enduring it, the victim won't share what they've been through at the hands of their partner with anyone. The abuser knows this. If the abuse is physical, and hospital treatment is required, the abuser may not let their victim get medical attention. This would take away their control over the victim and potentially lead to them being in a position where the victim chooses to end the relationship. As you may know, this is unlikely when you're trapped in a trauma bonded relationship, but it still weighs heavily on the mind of the abuser and fuels their behaviour. They will not let you go. Unless it's on their terms, of course, or they find a new victim to fuel their ego.

If they do let you seek medical treatment, they may accompany you to ensure you lie about how you sustained your injuries. They may even talk to the medical staff on your behalf. Although, it's highly unlikely a victim will unburden themselves to anyone outside of the relationship. Again, this threatens the partnership, something the victim does their best to avoid. By protecting the abuser at all costs, you're protecting the relationship. In turn, you're protecting yourself.

Whatever your incident may be can differ from time to time, too. One instance may have been direct physical abuse, the next may have been them verbally lashing out at you. Regardless, the fallout remains the same. You're beyond hurt - again. The pain you feel during this stage is almost unexplainable to those who have never endured it. It's not just the incident itself, either, it's the horrific aftermath you're left with.

You are left to pick up the pieces you didn't want smashed in the first place, likely both literally and figuratively. You will, invariably, be to blame for the incident, or your partners 'excuse' for the outburst will be a thinly veiled pointing of the finger towards you. You will need to lie to cover up your spouse's actions, to try to process the abuse you've just been put through, to try to pacify and calm your abuser, all the while maintaining a facade to the outside world. It's a burden we carry regardless of how much it grinds us down every time an incident occurs.

Phase 3: Reconciliation

Through all the pain, hurt, humiliation, and fear, we trudge on and pray for reconciliation. We are prepared to forget, or rather not mention, the horrific spate of tension and abuse we've been put through, just so our abuser will snap out of this episode and suggest reconciling.

Why would you want to reconcile with someone who treats you like that is a question asked by those ignorant to the complex trauma of Stockholm syndrome. We stay for many contradictory and difficult reasons rolled into one: security, comfort, financial stability, fear, too afraid of what the abuser will do if you leave... but the big reason few people understand is we stay out of love. We stay because we care. Because we can't imagine life without them.

Nine times out of ten, for me, I would instigate the reconciliation. I would beg, plead, and sob how I was sorry - despite sometimes not actually fully understanding what my offence was. Still, I just wanted respite, security and comfort, and for my partner to return to the loving person they were when we met (and could still be during calm periods in the relationship).

In the one out of ten instances where my partner would instigate the reconciliation, it would often be when he'd done something so terrible and unforgivable that he had no room to blame me. Even for someone as narcissistic as him, he knew when his gaslighting and lies were totally see through. So, in these cases, he would accept blame and insist he was misunderstood and his actions were a byproduct of 'poor mental health'. When I suggested seeking help for this, however, I was brushed aside. Sometimes he'd say he would get help for his actions, but he never followed through properly. False promises like this are, sadly, often the case in the reconciliation phase.

This part of the abuse cycle is like a relief to our anxiety and upset. It's like the sun coming out after a heavy period of rain.

Phase 4: Calm and Comfort is Restored

The love and adoration is back. At the very least, there's calm. Often the abuser will use this period to draw you back in, build up the trust they may have lost after the incident. You might find the abuser is being extra kind, perhaps even bringing gifts home or being extra affectionate. They might even apologise for their treatment of you.

When we're in the grasp of a trauma bond, we believe what our abuser tells us. We pray as hard as we can that this is the end - the abuse stops here. That they stay this way forever. We hope they mean it when they assure us it won't happen again. We are grateful that we've managed to keep the relationship intact because life without them is so unimaginable. We feel a plethora of emotions, and we are as in love as ever. But, the cycle doesn't stop. The rain cloud will - and always does - return.

Our abuser's love and attentiveness becomes colder and they turn distant. We seem to annoy them, and our presence can seem like it irritates them. Soon, they're picking up on our flaws and mistakes and point them out relentlessly. Yet again, we're in a position where we can't seem to do anything right.

From the hells of the incident, you felt like you'd recovered after reconciling. You thought you were both in love and happy again, and that the toxicity and abuse would fizzle out. Last time was the last time, right?

But the cycle keeps going. Now you're back at the tension-building phase. Again, you're walking on eggshells, afraid of what you may or may not do to trigger another eruption from your spouse. The timeframe from calmness to another bout of tension building isn't set in stone. You can endure a full cycle of abuse in the space of a week, going from phase one to four in a matter of days. You can also have prolonged periods of calmness before another event. Months could pass where you're lulled into a false sense of security. At my worst times, I went through the entire cycle multiple times in the same week.

From tension building all weekend to the incident occurring on a Monday, to reconciliation on Wednesday, to yet again more tension building on the Friday. Then nothing for months at a time. It's always going to happen though, even if we won't face up to that as a fact.

Why Do We Stay?

We try to rationalise why our relationship ended up this way. Is it something to do with us, with how we present ourselves? Did we trigger something in our abuser to create a breeding ground for their toxicity? Have we created a monster? Are we just needy and weak?

These are the kind of questions I used to ask myself before I was able to confront that I was enduring abuse because of my partner's toxic issues, not mine. When a compassionate, empathetic person meets a narcissist, it's a bad combination for a relationship. You aren't needy or weak, you're full of understanding and sensitivity. You're not a pushover, you're forgiving. You don't judge, but rather try to get to the root cause of your partner's behaviour. A toxic person will utilise these traits for their own gain.

Your kindness is made into a weakness. Your forgiveness is taken advantage of. Your abundance of love and patience is used against you. That's not to say these traits are weak - they are amazing attributes to have - but, as with a lot of good things in this world, they can be misused in the wrong hands.

It's hard when friends and family shake their heads when we return to our abuser. When they express bewilderment as to why we remain in such a toxic and abusive situation, we feel frustrated that they can't wrap their heads around our feelings. Even if the phrase 'Stockholm syndrome' is used, people often get it wrong: they think it's a case of a captor physically trapping their victim, refusing to let them go. In reality, often we're physically free to leave if we pick the right moment, but we're emotionally handcuffed to our spouse. We know we're suffering - but we can't bear being without them, even if it means a lifetime of suffering. Being trauma bonded means simply getting up and walking away isn't an option. We are the way we are because we've had to adapt to survive.

If you think back to the beginning of the relationship, it's likely you were very different from who you are now. Of course, your abuser wasn't the person they are now, either, but that's for a very different reason. They hid who they were until they could expose their true colours, knowing you'd not dare leave them at this point. You, however, have been shaped into the person you've become. To survive the emotional and perhaps physical abuse, you've developed strategies to help you cope. This means pleasing your partner by whatever means necessary, changing yourself to keep them appeased, going out of your way to avoid actions that will cause an incident, and protecting them at all costs.

But what stops us from saying, *enough is enough, I'm out*!

Like most aspects of a trauma bond, the answer is complex. There's no blanket reason we stay. We stay for a plethora of reasons; emotional, practical, financial. An abundance of fear.

We can often find it hard to put into words why we stay. I'll outline the reasons, other than the deep love and attachment you feel for your abuser, why we stay in toxic relationships, tightly held together by trauma and abuse. You may find you resonate with a number of these reasons, even if you've found it hard to rationalise in your head. Some may not be applicable to you, some may sound like your exact situation.

We stay because of the...

Threat to our physical and psychological well being

The threat from the abuser can be direct or indirect; either way, you know it's a threat, no matter how thinly veiled it is. When it's direct, the abuser can also threaten the well being of those close to you, such as family members. My ex threatened to smash my mother's windows if I dared return home, for example. He knew that would devastate me, so the grasp of control, using threats, worked. This type of behaviour ensures we understand the dynamic: that the safety of ourselves and our loved ones is somewhat secure if we comply.

Indirect threats work just as well. Subtle hints or assertive reminders that you can 'never leave' sit at the forefront of your mind. You'll get reminders that if you dare to leave, it won't be good. They can be vague about what will happen in this case, but the threat still hangs heavy over you. For example, your abuser may tell you tales of people that have wronged them, and explain how they exacted their revenge on those individuals. Knowing that your partner is vengeful by their own admission is an indirect threat. If your partner has exhibited violent behaviour but hasn't directly assaulted you, this is still abuse, and instilling fear and dread into you is a threat. If you dare upset them again, the violence could very well escalate to the direct target being you. A toxic spouse who smashes up belongings and household items and professes they'll never cross the line of direct assault is only one bout of anger away from doing so.

Intimidation is a big reason we don't leave, but to explain this to an outsider is often painful. Replies about safe-houses, the police, or shelters may come from a good place, but they fail to see that regardless of where we go, we are still fearful of our partner.

Small acts of kindness that lure us back into the trap

When we find ourselves in a frightening, threatening environment, it's human nature to seek out elements of hope. We have to seek out signs of improvement somehow, otherwise how would we keep going? We need hope to survive, even just a glimmer of it.

Abusers know this. They use this against us by offering us small acts of kindness - usually after a bout of abuse, but not always; it can happen when they feel their grip over us is slipping or that they need to love bomb us a little to fortify the cycle of abuse. This small gesture of kindness reminds us of the positive things we first fell for in our partner. It reminds us they are our source of comfort. In a hostage situation where the victim is suffering from Stockholm syndrome, things like being allowed food and water are considered acts of kindness from their abuser. It helps strengthen the bond between captor and victim.

In a relationship that's tied together with a trauma bond, small acts of kindness can be seen in the form of gifts, sweet words or compliments, or a thoughtful gesture. Sadly, it can also be seen when the abuser chooses not to abuse their victim: the victim will see this as proving their spouse is not 'that bad'. For example, you may do something to accidentally upset your partner. Past experience has told you what will happen; be it verbal abuse, silent treatment, or even physical abuse. However, when the anticipated bout of abuse doesn't occur, we breathe a sigh of relief and hold our abuser in higher esteem for not hurting us.

The views and perspective of the abuser are the only ones we're exposed to

It's not immediately obvious when you're in the trauma trap, but in order to secure our own safety and security, we adopt our abusers' perspective. Think of it this way: if you only have a few pennies to your name, your whole way of thinking revolves around your finances. The bulk of your decisions would be based on your lack of money. It's the same for an abusive relationship. You're primarily exposed to your partner's perspective, it's the only one you have. There is no other way of thinking.

It's a survival tactic, one that makes us agreeable and fiercely loyal to our abuser. In fact, we often cut off those on the outside who try to help us, or warn them to stop interfering in our relationship. We fear the repercussions should someone try to tear us from the situation we're in. We often block numbers, stop texts from coming through, change our number or ignore those who try to reach out to us and help. These well-meaning people don't see that in doing so, we see them as interfering and potentially rocking the boat. This would be incredibly bad for us. For me, I had to blank my own mother's calls, even blocking her on occasion to secure my own safety. I would get frustrated and angry at her if she called at the wrong time, causing me to endure rants and accusations from my abuser.

Of course, we didn't see the situation clearly at the time. We don't see these individuals trying to help us as well-meaning, we see them as nuisances. We are more aligned with our abuser's perspective, not the truth. We stay because we've been brainwashed.

Extreme emotional investment we've put into our partner

We've spent so much time trying to 'fix' our partner, endured countless hours of hurt, humiliation and pain, and we are relentlessly committed. Not to mention, all of the tears shed over our partner. If we suddenly dare to abandon the relationship, all of this would have been for nought. It's the sunk cost fallacy, except we don't realise the price we pay for being in the relationship is far, far heavier than any of the perceived benefits.

Plus, even though we've been degraded, treated like dirt, and been made to feel like we're worthless, we still have a small smidgen of pride. The embarrassment to admit to those who've tried to help us that they were right all along feels too difficult to suffer.

On top of that, we are intertwined in every way with our partner. We have a home, bills, commitments, maybe even children. We have built a life with them and we can't bear to shatter everything we've been working towards. We are incredibly invested in this relationship, our whole world revolves around it. The idea that we tear ourselves apart from it, regardless of how constantly hurt the partnership makes us, is unbearable. To be without the person we love and who can offer us occasional comfort isn't fathomable.

Financial investment is too great to escape

In the huge power differential of a toxic relationship, finances are often complex. Not complex for the abuser, but most certainly complex for the victim. In many cases, we have little to no access to any meaningful financial resources. This could be when the abuser withholds money or strips you of your own money. They could have everything in their name, meaning you're stripped of both money and control. It could also be that you're the main breadwinner and the abuser has put you in a difficult financial situation. Perhaps you find yourself in a position of not being able to afford life on your own without your abuser. Living with Stockholm syndrome often means enduring multiple forms of abuse, one of them frequently being financial abuse.

My ex would know exactly what I earned, and I had to account for every penny. If I had surplus money, which was anything left over after covering the bills, I was to spend it on something that my partner wanted. A new TV that we 'needed', an expensive bottle of alcohol, takeaway food, a new computer... anything my ex could think of to fritter away any extra money in my bank, he would insist we have it.

He earned more than me, yet often contributed less to these luxury purchases. This left him in the beneficial position of having these nice things but also having a nice savings pot in his bank account. I, on the other hand, lived month to month, often struggling to get by for those last two weeks of the month. I had to use overdrafts and loans to simply get to work and back and eat, which caused me further financial stress. I didn't see it then, but it's clear now what my ex was doing: ensuring I had no means to leave him. No little cushion of money to escape him and see me through. Not even enough money for a bus ticket. Abusive partners can also take out credit in their victims name. Credit cards, loans, and store cards may be maxed out with the victim left to pay the monthly bill. This also serves the same purpose: to strip you of your resources.

It can also go the other way, too. The abuser makes sure they have control over everything; the car, the bank account, the house, the budgeting. This creates a huge gap in control, with the victim needing the abuser for basic survival. Food, shelter and comfort are all at the behest of the abuser. Even if the controlled spouse has a joint account with their partner, they may not have access to the account details, or the PIN. Asking for access to these things is often akin to simply asking for a bout of abuse to occur.

Intimacy and the way our abuser uses it against us

There's no denying, we've given just about everything we can to our abuser. Our self-worth, our self-esteem, our confidence, and our emotional and physical intimacy. It's not uncommon for a narcissistic, toxic partner to use intimate details or pictures against their victim and hold it over them as a tool to keep them in the relationship. They threaten to spread these personal things on the internet and disclose confidential information to friends and family to humiliate their partner. The threat of rumours and lies about you also prevent you from taking steps to remove yourself from the situation; it's just too much of a risk, you feel. It's best to endure the grasp of the abuser rather than face the judgement of the world. The abuser knows you feel this way, which is why their manipulation works. When you're entangled in a toxic relationship with a manipulative person, blackmail can often become so prevalent that we see it as the norm.

This leads me on to the next reason...

Fear

Fear is why we stay.

Different kinds of fear all rolled into one. Fear of the threats they make. Fear of how your abuser will cope without you. Fear of the unknown. Fear of starting again. Fear of looking over your shoulder wherever you go. Fear for your family's safety. Fear of the lies and the smear campaign that would tarnish your name.

Above all else, we stay because we're frozen with fear.

It's hard to verbalise this fear or to articulate it enough for outsiders to understand. To them, we are contradicting ourselves. We are fearful of our partner, yet can't live without them and are worried about their wellbeing should we end the relationship? *Makes no sense*, I've heard people scoff.

When I tried to explain myself to those who questioned why I was still in an abusive relationship (and I still didn't know about Stockholm syndrome or trauma bonding), I often offered up contradictory reasons like this. You can imagine the responses I got. Disbelief, strange looks, suspicious follow-up questions and victim-blaming often ensued. Responses like this just pushed me further towards my abuser. Nobody else understood. I felt safer there despite it being a place of great danger. At least he understood.

Looking back now, it's clear a lot of individuals just didn't understand the human reaction to an emotionally distressing situation (which puts your mental and emotional safety in jeopardy, not to mention the danger of physical abuse).

They can't, or won't, digest the fact that when we're exposed to a traumatic experience, we don't think logically. We can't process information coherently. Imagine you're being chased by a hungry wolf, baring its teeth and snapping at your heels; you'd be running as fast as you could, only thinking about your safety. You wouldn't be thinking about getting groceries or wondering what movie you'd like to watch that evening. You would be doing whatever you needed to protect yourself. It's the same when you're trapped in a relationship with an abuser.

That's another reason why enduring a toxic relationship that is tightly stitched together by a trauma bond is so isolating and lonely: people just don't understand. It's so complex and inconsistent that they don't wrap their heads around it. 'As soon as my husband raises his fist to me is the day I leave,' one of my friends used to say. 'I don't get why people stay in abusive relationships'. These comments pushed me further away from her, and the possibility of confiding in her, and closer to my abuser.

Incredulous friends see us staying silent and isolating ourselves further. Fear, guilt, and the idea we are doubted consume us, and become the walls in which we find ourselves trapped.

You'll know just how wily and masterful your abuser is when it comes to coercing you with love bombing, too. 'If you ever loved me you'd never leave'. The abuser knows just how dependent and attached you are to them, and they know just how hurtful it is for you when they threaten to hurt themselves. Threats of them harming themselves should we ever leave seems to hurt us just as much as direct threats to our safety. My ex would assure me he'd take a whole box of pills if I ever left and leave a note to make sure everyone knew why: because of me. The idea of him not being around anymore was overwhelming, and he'd make me imagine a world without him in it knowing I just couldn't bear the thought. I'd be overcome with guilt, despite me not actually doing anything wrong in the first instance.

Then there were the threats of calling my employer to make me lose my job, to tell everyone I was a psycho, to make sure I was never left alone for as long as I lived. You hear these things repeatedly and you know the abusive lengths your spouse will go to, then you tend to heed these threats.

When you have direct abuse from your partner coupled with cynical folk doubting your reality, you have a dangerous combination. Add in the eroding away of your self-esteem and ability to rationalise, this creates the abuser's compliant, subservient prey. And they wouldn't have it any other way.

The Posttraumatic Impact Stockholm Syndrome Has

Trauma and PTSD go hand in hand. You don't endure a toxic relationship and escape unscathed. Many of the things you've been taught by your abuser have to be unlearned and there's a lot of work on your thought pattern and self-esteem to be done. Much of this is to help you deal with the posttraumatic stress you're left with. When you eventually flee the abusive situation you're in, you're not suddenly absolved of the trauma. It's still there, but at least when you're away from your abuser, you can begin to work on undoing the damage they've caused.

While abusive relationships aren't 'all bad' - in the sense that there are moments where the abuser is loving and affectionate towards their victim - the entire time is a traumatic event to your brain. Your mind views it all as one, big dangerous event. We are living in traumatic purgatory while in the relationship with our abuser, and when we eventually flee from our abuser, the trauma remains.

The memories of hurtful events, horrible bouts of abuse, earth-shattering lies and toxic behaviour repeats in our mind like a broken record. Ironically, our brain does this on purpose to protect us from possible future danger, preparing us for the next traumatising event so we can better shield ourselves from the hurt. While our brain is doing its best to stop us from repeating the same traumatic events, the awful memories are stuck at the forefront of our mind, making us feel incredibly anxious and emotionally still in pain.

You may not think you have PTSD; I certainly didn't even after I fled my abuse. I knew I was damaged, but I mistakenly thought PTSD was reserved for those who'd been to war or endured a particularly traumatic car crash. I didn't correlate how I was feeling with posttraumatic stress, I just thought I was heartbroken and needed to find a way to put the pieces back together. It turns out I was half right; I did need to put the pieces back together, but it wasn't just the heartbreak I was enduring. It was PTSD.

Suffering posttraumatic stress isn't something that happens only when you're out of the relationship; it most certainly starts while you're in the midst of abuse and escalates the more traumatic things you're exposed to. However, for me and many others who've experienced a trauma bond, the PTSD ramps up when you leave the partnership. The disorder rears its head in a number of ways that I'll discuss. Just to note, PTSD sufferers don't necessarily exhibit all of the symptoms outlined below, but generally they do display most of them. Perhaps you'll notice some of these have creeped their way into your existence as a result of the trauma you've endured.

PTSD symptom #1: Hypervigilance

This is your brain trying to shield you from traumatic, threatening situations. Hypervigilance in small doses is healthy. For example, if we're walking home late one night and we take a detour through a back alley to shorten the walk, we may find ourselves in a state of hypervigilance. We are very aware of potential threats that lurk in the shadows, and we are on high alert to ensure we can flee any possible attack. It serves to protect us. However, chronic hypervigilance is different: it consumes the individual, causing them to have an abnormal startle reflex and leaves them feeling a sense of danger a lot of the time.

People with PTSD as a result of abuse - spousal or otherwise - tend to be chronically hypervigilant. They are jumpy and often react quickly to their environment, such as hearing a door close loudly. They're also extremely quick to react to their perception of comments or statements from other people. For example, some polite feedback from a co-worker may be taken as an attack by someone who is hypervigilant, because they're so used to being verbally attacked by their spouse and are always waiting for the next negative interaction.

Being in this heightened state of anxiety can also mean the sufferer avoids doing day-to-day things for fear of threat. That could mean keeping away from the store to avoid interactions with others, not driving anywhere for fear of being a target of road rage or not answering the door in case there's danger on the other side. Everything is perceived as a threat, and in some cases, this turns into the sufferer not leaving the house at all. This, to them, limits the possibility of ending up in a scenario that's traumatic or difficult to escape.

Hypervigilance does impact quality of life, there's no denying it. Relaxing seems unattainable; real relaxation, anyway. While you may have moments where you feel at peace, you're more often than not in a heightened state of perpetual panic when you're prone to hypervigilance. Sleeping when you're in a panicked state like this is also out of the question, and if you do drift off, chances are you dream (or, more likely, have nightmares) about the very thing you're worried about. This feeling of being on edge all of the time surely impacts our mood and our ability to think straight. When we feel backed into a corner like this, outbursts and fits of anger can cause us to act without truly thinking things through.

Holding conversations with others also proves to be a mean feat when we're in a state of hypervigilance. We find we can't retain information well, unable to muster up thoughtful replies or contributions to the conversation, or think clearly enough to engage with the other person. Add to this, being in this perpetually ready state for danger means we're incredibly suspicious and mistrustful of people, making it hard for us to feel we have anywhere to turn. Except for our abuser, that is.

In scientific terms, hypervigilance is triggered by epinephrine, otherwise known as adrenaline. People who are hypervigilant have sustained levels of this stress hormone, which also causes increased blood pressure and heart rate.

If any of this sounds like you, then there are techniques you can use to help bring yourself back down from the heightened state of anxiety. When you're feeling hypervigilance creeping up, take a moment to be still, and breathe in deeply and out slowly. This will allow room for the brain fog to clear a little; enough for you to try to rationalise the thing or things you're anxious or afraid of. Try to find an objective reason why you're feeling the way you do. If you find clear evidence that your heightened state is warranted, take a moment before acting upon it. Anxiety causes fight-or-flight responses, but you need to pause at this point to acknowledge your fear, why it's there, and understand it's your brain's way of looking out for you. Knee-jerk reactions are a sure-fire sign of hypervigilance, so use this mindful moment to avoid snap decisions. You'll be amazed how we can logicise our feelings when we give ourselves time to do so.

PTSD symptom #2: Flashbacks and Intrusive Thoughts

I've coupled flashbacks and intrusive thoughts as one symptom, even though they are two separate byproducts of trauma and PTSD. This is because one often leads into the other; an unwanted, invasive thought could enter your mind, which triggers flashbacks to a particularly nasty episode of abuse.

You've probably heard of intrusive thoughts at some point. They're actually fairly common and most people do have them at points throughout their life. However, for a person with PTSD as a result of trauma, these thoughts jump into our mind without warning and repeat as if they're on a loop. It can often be a replaying of things we've endured or seen, as if that memory is sitting at the forefront of our mind ready to drop in and traumatise us further whenever it likes. Reliving episodes of abuse when we do our best to often suppress the memory is a whole trauma of its own.

I would often get the same intrusive thought about my ex laughing. Out of nowhere, I'd get a picture in my mind's eye of my ex smiling and chuckling away. The laugh was smug, evil, and condescending. The kind of laugh that was reserved for episodes of gaslighting and crazy making.

This would then invariably lead to a flashback of the time I confronted him about cheating on me. I had almost concrete evidence, yet he still denied it to me, smirking and laughing as he rebuffed my proof. This day hurt me deeply, and his reaction to my hurt only twisted the knife further. Whenever I got this intrusive thought, this flashback would invariably follow. As much as I tried to wipe my mind's eye clean and try and force myself to think of something new, it would loop over and over again.

Flashbacks and unwanted thoughts can strike at any time, anyplace, like we're powerless to defeat the hold our abuser has over us, even in our own brain. For me, flashbacks became more prevalent (as did hypervigilance) in the first year after I left my abuser, but they were also present throughout the relationship too. The most difficult time in dealing with them was when I was out of the toxicity of the relationship, something that frustrated me greatly.

On top of this, you might find that certain smells or sounds even trigger a flashback. I recall one advert on TV that played while I endured an episode of abuse: every time it came on afterwards, I had to knock it off or walk out of the room. It brought on the most painful flashbacks that made me sick to my stomach, so I avoided it as best I could. Flashbacks make us feel stuck in that horrible moment in time, distressing us and leaving us feeling anger, fear, upset and grief.

To better cope with these unsettling and unwanted thoughts and memories, prevention is the best deterrent. You need to know the triggers in order to avoid them, or at the very least limit your interaction with those triggers (like I did with the TV advert).

If you're prone to flashbacks or episodes of intrusive thinking, try and think back to what you were feeling and what was on your mind directly before the episode. Was there something you were thinking about specifically? Could this be a possible trigger? Take your time to try to identify early warning signs - this will help you ground yourself before the flashback gets a hold of you.

To 'ground' yourself simply means making yourself be present. Let me guide you in doing this. As an aside, grounding yourself works for a number of anxiety-related symptoms, so it's a great mental asset to learn.

In order to stay in the present and not be dragged into unwanted thoughts, first of all take an inventory of your surroundings. The books on your shelf, the ornaments, the candles, the magazines on the coffee table, the bottle of water next to your feet... identify what is directly around you. When you do this, you are in the moment, not being washed away into memories.

Manage your surrounding sounds, too, if you can. Put music on, the type you wouldn't normally play. It will distract you, especially if you've never heard it before and it's unfamiliar.

Get your other senses present, too. Smell and touch can help you greatly when you're keeping yourself present. Smell something strong, like mint. Take a walk outside, freshly cut grass and flowers also work. Grab a cold block of ice - that one is always sure to keep you in the moment. The longer you can keep yourself from slipping into flashbacks, the more you're present, the harder it is for the nasty thoughts to creep in.

PTSD symptom #3: Trouble Concentrating

Those suffering from PTSD frequently struggle to concentrate, even on everyday things. Mundane things like grabbing groceries become stressful as you leave your credit card at home, you forget to pay bills on time, you don't take in what people are saying and you struggle to follow the storyline of the movie you're watching. This is also known as brain fog.

This is a direct result of being overloaded with anxiety, and it's not that you're suffering memory loss or aren't good at retaining information; it's that your mind is overworked from the trauma you're enduring.

When you have PTSD, your brain is unable to function optimally. I'll explain how this works: PTSD affects two parts of the brain, the amygdala and the prefrontal cortex. The amygdala (the cells located near the base of the brain) serves to detect possible threats and is an activator for the nervous system. The prefrontal cortex helps us choose what actions we take over the detection of threats. It's a complex brain function that regulates our emotions and helps us solve problems efficiently. These two parts of the brain go into overdrive when we're exposed to trauma, rendering us unable to think clearly.

Brain fog sees the sufferer become detached from what's going on around them, not truly taking in what's happening in the present moment. They may seem on the outside to be in their own little world, when really they're mentally fatigued. To take in simple information is a real task for someone whose mind is clouded by fog. It also affects the sufferer physically, even a good night's rest doesn't stop the individual feeling fatigued and groggy.

I lived in this hazy state for such a long time. I truly wasn't present a lot of the time, which equates to years lost to trauma and the symptoms of abuse. To think back, I was just on autopilot, although this just served to exacerbate all of the other symptoms I was enduring. It's these lesser-known symptoms of PTSD that really rob you of your life, so the sooner you can pinpoint them, the quicker you can take actions to rectify them by working to break the trauma bond.

PTSD symptom #4: Dissociation

Dissociation is when you lose touch with reality, either intermittently or on a consistent basis. It's a disconnection from your experiences, thoughts, history, and even who you are as a person. You begin to tear yourself away from who you are and it's almost like you're merely enduring life with no identity.

The way this symptom rears its head differs from person to person, but the reason it happens is always the same: to distance yourself from the traumatic and disturbing experiences and memories you wish to escape. It may come and go, as it did with me, or some people go years and years in a dissociative state.

Poor grasp on reality, denial of traumatic events occurring, gaps in the memory and erratic behaviour are all symptoms of dissociation. When a sufferer is going through this phase, they may seem like they're not really there. Like the lights are on but nobody's home, as my dad used to say. Life feels surreal, yet feels like nothing at all, is the best way I can explain it. If you've gone through a dissociative phase, you can perhaps relate. It's incredibly dream-like, like the dreams you have that make no sense but while you're in them you don't question what's going on. You just go with it.

Essentially what's happened is you've detached from yourself emotionally, which also means detaching from your self-awareness, memory and consciousness. This serves as a self-preservation tactic to stop us feeling so much hurt and emotional torment. We need calmness in our mind, and we figure the best way to do this is by pulling our emotional plug temporarily.

It's our instinct to adopt these survival techniques in situations that are emotionally and mentally crippling, and it can help us get through some of the darkest days of our lives. Ideally, however, we'd never need to regress into this state of being at the hands of our toxic partner, but our brain does what it needs to when we're exposed to emotional maltreatment.

PTSD symptom #5: Nightmares

We need sleep to restore ourselves. A good night's sleep is key for our mind and body to function optimally, rejuvenating itself as we are in a relaxed state. However, PTSD sees that we're rarely in a state of relaxation, and as a result, our sleep patterns are disrupted, and nightmares often plague the little sleep we do get. Most people who have PTSD suffer from nightmares, which are undeniably distressing both while asleep and when we wake up.

It's almost like our abuser has been forever etched into our mind, and the episodes of abuse come back to haunt us even when we're unconscious. It's been theorised that dreams serve to help us store memories, which makes sense; we seem to have the most horrific dreams when we're enduring an emotionally gruelling time. These real-feeling nightmares don't just replay events that we've gone through, they can often take them to terrifying new heights, adding on new horrors as they unfold.

When we wake up from these night terrors, often with a jolt, we struggle to differentiate our bad dreams from reality. When we eventually realise the ordeal was just a nightmare, albeit born from true experiences, we still struggle to shake off the panic and dread we're left with. The entire days that follow are like a daze as we come to terms with the things we saw and felt in our dream.

The effects of a trauma bond go much further than we can truly comprehend while we're in the midst of an abusive relationship. In fact, the effects of PTSD are often things our abuser berates us for or mocks us about, despite the fact that they're the very reason these symptoms present themselves in the first place.

This leads me onto another side-effect of Stockholm syndrome: learned helplessness. I've touched upon this slightly earlier in the book, but it's a complex aspect of an abusive relationship, which I'll cover in more depth in the following chapter.

Unlearning Learned Helplessness

Learned helplessness happens to us without us even knowing. It's a result of our abuser constantly drip feeding us with negativity and exposing us to traumatic scenarios. We've learned that we have to endure these bouts of abuse because we don't feel there is any other option. We can't leave, we can't fight the bad episodes, we can't compromise or talk things through. We simply have to endure. We are helpless.

We weren't born with this defeatist way of thinking, though. We've been conditioned to feel this way by our abuser.

In 1965, an experiment into learned helplessness was carried out by Dr. Martin Seligman. Like with most experiments done years ago, it was carried out on animals, specifically dogs for this experiment. I must add, I wince at the idea of cruelty inflicted on animals for the sake of 'science', but this analysis into learned helplessness was carried out many years ago. Although I disagree with the acts carried out in the experiment, I'm mentioning it here because it offers an easy-to-understand explanation of learned helplessness.

The experiment saw Dr. Seligman ring a bell, after which he would give the dogs a light shock. After repeating this multiple times, it was observed that the dogs would react to the imminent shock before it had even been given. As soon as the dogs heard the bell, they'd react as if they'd already been shocked.

The next part of the experiment is where the term 'learned helplessness' was born.

Dr. Seligman then placed each dog in the experiment in their own crate next to one another, which was separated by a small divider. Should the dog wish, it could hop into the crate next to it. The floor on some crates was electrified. The floor next door to those crates wasn't. Electric shocks were then administered to the chosen floors, and Dr. Seligman fully expected the affected dogs to hop into the crates next to them. To his surprise, they didn't. They simply laid down on the floor that was giving them shocks. The dogs had learned that nothing they did would prevent the shocks from occurring, so they endured them until they stopped. Dr. Seligman coined the phrase 'learned helplessness' to describe the dogs' behaviour of not trying to escape their traumatic situation due to past experience training them that they're helpless to do so.

It just so happens that in this instance, we're not too different from these dogs. Humans work in the same way when it comes to learned helplessness. We've been trained by our abuser that there's no escape, no way to flee the relationship without immense pain and suffering, and no way to stop the inevitable cycle of abuse repeating itself. We've been conditioned to feel how we feel, just like the dogs were in the experiment. When we please our partner, we repeat those acts because we've been rewarded with kindness. Likewise, when we're punished for upsetting them or disobeying them, we do our best to avoid repeating those acts.

The good news is we can decondition ourselves. The first part of breaking the toxic bond is unlearning this helpless thought pattern. It takes a bit of work and mindfulness, and you may struggle to always implement the methods I'll go on to describe, but it's important that you work to unlearn the feelings of helplessness and dependency you've been conditioned to feel.

When I was in the process of learning about the toxic relationship I was in, a lot of the information I was reading offered advice on how to change my thinking, as that was touted as the first step in breaking the trauma bond. For such a long time, I rolled my eyes at the idea of it, brushing it off as self-help gurus giving generic advice with flowery writing. I didn't want to become mindful or 'be more optimistic', I wanted to be free of the pain and toxic attachment I had to my partner. It was only when I realised that no amount of reading about abusive relationships would help unless I changed my pattern of thinking that things began to improve for me. Let me explain how to reframe your thoughts when dealing with the negativity of your situation.

The ABC Method

This method helped me immensely when I eventually let myself give it a go. In fact, I still use it to this day to help me process and rationalise events that are hurtful or difficult. Perhaps, like I did at first, you may dismiss this as 'psychobabble' or fluffy optimism, but keep it in mind, regardless. If you don't implement it straight away, at least you have the knowledge of it to come back to and execute when you're ready.

The ABC Method is you offering yourself a more flexible mental response to trauma and disappointment, and is a way for you to unlearn the defeatist mindset of learned helplessness. Upon reading and applying it, you might even think of it as simplistic: and it is. However, this technique forces you to do something that doesn't come naturally while in the midst of abuse: think clearly.

While it's called The ABC Method, the letters actually go all the way to E. Let me outline them all:

A is for Adversity

The first thing you need to do is describe the adversity in a detached way. Take emotion out of the equation. For example, after an episode where your spouse was rageful, you could say, 'I was yelled at and now my partner is refusing to speak to me.' There is no evaluation of the situation, no emotional statements. It's a pragmatic look at the hurtful situation you've endured. Stating only the facts can be hard to do when you're fraught with upset and anxiety, but it's something that gets easier the more you practice.

B is for Belief

Next you need to process how you interpreted the abusive episode. Don't think about how you wish your partner had behaved or what you should or shouldn't have said during the incident. Clearly outline how the negative interaction was interpreted by you. An example could be, 'My partner yelled that I was a burden to him. Now he's not talking to me. This is usually a sign that he's going to be hostile for the next few days until he's satisfied with my apologies.' Again, no emotion, just interpretation based on your interaction with your partner and prior experience of similar situations.

C is for Consequence

Now it's time to reflect on the feelings arising from your beliefs. You need to be a bit more introspective for this portion of the thinking process, retracing your emotional reaction to the trauma you've endured. For example, you might think, 'I'm full of frustration that my partner wouldn't hear my side and calls me names. I'm angry that he does this then refuses to speak to me for days on end. When he called me a burden I felt angry, but I couldn't express this because he would then blame me for the whole argument. Now I feel like I ought to apologise just to get things back to normal'. This section allows you to delve into the aftermath of the negative interaction, going over how you felt and reacted to the toxic scenario.

D is for Disputation

Here you can dispute your reactions to the abusive event. Perhaps, after processing the bout of abuse bit by bit in your head, you begin to reconcile that saying sorry (while feeling it may speed up the timeline of abuse to reconciliation quicker) isn't something you should do. While it's natural to want the silent treatment to end, unlearning the things you're conditioned to do is a big part of breaking the trauma bond. Giving yourself the time to think about your automated responses to the abuse is a good opportunity to make small steps towards rectifying those responses.

E is for Energization

This part is putting into action your findings from the disputation stage. Whatever you figured out was wrong in your reaction or response to the abuse needs to be put into action. Have you realised apologising is just working to keep the abuser in a place of dominance? Then refrain from doing so. Does your abuser relish in you getting angry, and uses your outburst of frustration against you? Then you need to stop that moving forward.

That's The ABC Method, developed by the same person who carried out the shock experiment on dogs, Dr. Martin Seligman. It's fundamentally simple, but logic and rationale aren't our strong points when we're in a toxic situation. We often need reminding how to process information in a healthy way, and the regular use of this method helps to shift your perspective of the abusive scenarios you're exposed to. Too often, we stew in our heartache and upset, only thinking of the things we can do to restore calm and make our spouse love us again. With The ABC Method, emotions are stripped from the pattern of thinking and replaced by fact. This helps you reframe the abuse and stops you from wallowing in helplessness. The only thing you can control is you, and that's what this method serves to remind you. Regular use of this way of thinking sets the foundations for a less helpless way of thinking.

I understand you're perhaps not ready to up and leave your partner. A trauma bond is deep-rooted and undeniably tight, so I know that's not an immediate option. However, at some point, you'll find yourself in a position where you know you need to leave. It'll hurt, I can't deny that, but it'll be the beginning of a brand new chapter, and the heartache doesn't last. In order to get to that point, we need to weaken the bond, which I'll discuss in the next chapter, and mentally prepare yourself for detachment, which I'll discuss now.

Throughout all of this I want you to remember: you control nothing but yourself. You can't, and never will be able to, control the behaviour of your spouse, or anyone else for that matter. You can't stop the cycle, you can't circumvent it and you can't prevent your abuser from treating you the way they do. Remove all thoughts of trying to control anything except yourself. You are in control of you. Research has shown that those who feel like they have no control over their lives and are unable to change their situation have low self-efficacy. This tightens the invisible tether that connects you to your abuser.

To remedy this, you need to make an effort to shift your mindset away from what you can't control to what you can control. Pessimism tends to be your general world view when you're in an abusive relationship, and this needs to change. Of course, it's hard to see life as rainbows and sunshine when our spouse is willfully harming us, but it goes deeper than that. It's about shifting your way of thinking. As is, a person dealing with the trauma of abuse tends to think negatively with the 'three p's'. Let me explain what these are.

Personal

This is where you perceive any difficult or hurtful events that happen as your fault. Everything bad that happens is personally your fault, or happened because of something you triggered. Negative experiences and situations happen to and around you because of you.

Of course, this isn't true. When you're with an individual who lets you take the blame for any unfortunate or negative events, your ability to be logical is all but stomped out. Your outlook is bleak, your self-perception is at an all-time low, and you're constantly blaming yourself for any bad things going on around you.

Pervasive

Bad experiences are viewed as seeping over into every aspect of your life. This way of thinking sees the victim believe their situation is pervasive, and all areas of their life are impacted by their situation. This promotes feelings of helplessness and ensures the victim resigns themselves to the abuse.

Permanent

The victim views their way of living as permanent. While they still have glimmers of hope that their spouse will reform and refrain from abusing them moving forward, they accept their lifestyle as permanent and don't truly believe their situation will improve.

It's upsetting to think back to when I was with my ex and my whole thought pattern was negative. The three p's engulfed my mind, not a positive thought in sight. Of course, I had a little bit of hope, and prayed that my situation would change, but I didn't truly believe it was feasible. It was a nice thought, not a realistic one. How wrong I was.

If you find you're stuck in this negative way of thinking, you need to recognise when this happens and reframe your thought. If you're always blaming yourself for bad things happening, take a moment and rationalise. Outside forces that we have no control over often cause unfortunate things to happen. Consider that you're not to blame for things outside of your control. People's reactions are not things you can take the blame for. Other people's behaviour isn't something you can ever be blamed for.

You need to think the opposite of the three p's.

Turn *personal to impersonal*. 'I make my partner so mad, I can't do anything right,' is a personal way to think. Shift that: 'My partner has control and anger issues, and will become rageful when I do something he perceives as wrong'. Tailor this to your own situation.

Does your partner tell you they find you pathetic? *Reframe* that, don't *accept* that. They're taking your abundance of emotion and feelings for them and turning into something hurtful and negative. You're not pathetic. Whatever events or situations you take and place blame on yourself, take some time to consider making it impersonal.

Don't be *pervasive, be specific*. Your relationship feels like it creates a black cloud over your head that follows you everywhere. You feel anything you try your hand at is a massive struggle and a certain failure. Perhaps things aren't going well in other aspects of your life and you think that's all down to that prevalent dark cloud hanging over you. Remember, though: you are in control of you. That metaphorical black cloud refers to your relationship, not you as a person.

Permanent becomes temporary. Nothing lasts forever. Even the darkest of nights are sure to see the sunrise. Your situation feels never-ending, like the chains won't ever be broken. I fully understand the thinking that your situation won't get better, but it certainly can't stay the same. What would become of you if it did?

Change is an inevitable part of life. 'I'll never be able to find the strength to leave, I can't bear to be without my partner,' may be a recurring thought pattern of yours. Again, reframe that.

While you may not have that strength at the moment, remember, you're reading this book. You're seeking out information about your situation and are actively seeking ways to better it. 'I may not have the strength to leave now, but

I know I deserve better and I know things can be better,' is a much healthier, and more logical, way to think of your situation. You're also offering yourself the idea that one day, you'll find your strength. The more you repeat that to yourself, the quicker that day comes.

In the battle against learned helplessness, positive reinforcement is a huge factor in beating the beast. The idea of thinking positively about yourself may not come naturally. This is where positive reinforcement can help. Any kind of positive feedback serves to help your self-esteem, and that's exactly what you're going to offer yourself.

You don't always need other people to offer you positive reinforcement, although this works as well (but, you can't rely on this as a source of esteem-boosting - you need to do that for yourself). For example, if you're having a horrible time with your partner and their actions are particularly difficult for you to endure at the moment, someone telling you how great at your job is would serve as an esteem pick-me-up. Your self-worth would see a small boost: if others can see your worth, why can't your partner? Perhaps you do deserve better, could be your thought pattern after such an interaction.

However, we can't predict or control what others say about us or to us. We can only control ourselves (you might notice a recurrence of that phrase through this book - I want it to be your new mantra). So, we will give positive reinforcement to ourselves. Think back to past events, specifically ones that made you feel the most helpless. Initially, you might view those episodes as you being weak, provoking, difficult, or even deserving of the abuse you suffered. Reevaluate it.

You reframe your past actions in a positive way. Instead of thinking back to a time where you didn't stick up for yourself when you were being verbally abused, be proud of yourself for acting in a way that best preserved your safety. While the interaction angered and upset you, you chose not to rise to the goading or inner rage you felt and avoided further abuse. Give yourself acknowledgement and kudos for that. Perhaps you think back to a time where people have tried to step in and save you from the relationship and you were hurtful to them for intruding. This memory may make you think you're nasty, unkind, mean spirited and selfish. Go back to that moment and be the empathy and reinforcement you need. Every interaction you have had is positive, because you can learn from it and do better in the future.

Don't beat yourself up, you know yourself there are people in this world who would relish in you thinking so negatively of yourself. You have to be your own advocate, even if that starts internally at first. Champion yourself.

Breaking The Toxic Bond

This is likely the part of the book you dread applying to real life. Before I dive into breaking the trauma bond, let me say that I don't expect you to read this chapter and immediately apply it to your life. Not right away, anyway. It takes time. I think, for me, it took around a year or so before I implemented any of the advice or information I'd been reading into. I left multiple times, but I was always sucked back into the cycle of abuse, never fully escaping until I left the relationship with one clear thought: I can't ever go back.

My point is, leaving isn't a once and done thing. Very (and I must stress *very*) rarely does a victim of abuse leave the relationship for the first time and never go back.

Even when I knew I had to leave my abuser, I was still trying to find a way to make life easier with him without having to face the heartache of detaching myself from him. Perhaps during this time, I was readying myself for the imminent break-up; something I didn't fully want, but something I knew had to happen or I'd be stuck in purgatory forever. Still, I was armed with a wealth of information that proved invaluable when I eventually took the plunge and fled the relationship. If you're reading this, it looks like you already know you need to leave, but feel unable to. You're in a good mental position to work on severing the trauma bond because you know you have to.

I promise you the life you can have without the toxicity, hurt and pain is worth the initial heartache you feel when you flee your abuser. Imagine a life where you have an abundance of strong connections with numerous people, the ability to go places and do things without fear, and pursue the things that make you happy? Even if you don't know what makes you happy yet, you need to escape your abuser in order to find out what that is. You do not get happiness from your abuser. You get moments of comfort and familiarity from them. It's a case of better the devil you know, which is something many of us are willing to accept when we're so devoid of self-esteem.

When I was reading up on how to leave my abuser years ago, a lot of the advice was completely inapplicable to me. *Work on your career, focus on yourself, make friends outside of the relationship...* None of this was helpful for me. A lot of it suggested getting yourself into a confident position where you felt able to leave the relationship because you loved yourself enough to do so. I think it works the other way around. You leave the relationship broken, without self-esteem, few friends or contacts and harbouring the heavy weights of trauma and PTSD. There is no way you can work on your self-esteem while you're perpetually being re-traumatised and abused. You're at your lowest when you leave. But, when you're at rock bottom, the only way is up.

The first thing you need to do is physically separate yourself from your abuser. This is non-negotiable. Perhaps you've left before and returned to your partner because you couldn't imagine life without them. I did that multiple times. The closer I was to leaving for good, the longer the separation period would be. The time I left prior to ending it for good lasted a whole month.

However, during this period I hadn't cemented it in my brain that I would never go back to the relationship. I was able to block my ex and refrain from reaching out to them (which had previously been quite a mean feat). I was still, even if just a little, emotionally open to them. I hadn't been strict enough with myself, and as a result, went back to the relationship for another hellish four months. I could have used those four months to work on myself and build myself back up from the ashes. Instead, I was once again engulfed in the trauma bond, wondering how I was going to carry on if this was the rest of my life.

To physically remove yourself from your abusive situation creates a space for you to emotionally detach yourself from your abuser. The physical separation comes first, the emotional attachment severs afterwards. It doesn't happen overnight; you don't suddenly stop yearning for them after being without them for a week. You will want to run back to them, to reach out, to give things another chance. You just want to be with them. You need to be incredibly strict with yourself when you leave. You left for good, you need to keep reminding yourself. A trauma bond is like an addiction to your abuser, and you are going through withdrawals.

Think about an addict trying to go cold turkey with their drug of choice. They don't wake up one morning and decide they want to get clean and then simply flush their stash down the toilet. They have to endure the restlessness, the sleepless nights, the nausea, and the emotionally painful effects of withdrawal before they can find themselves again. Just like we need to do in order to flush the abuser from our system. I can't deny this period feels like suffering, but it's a necessary evil we need to endure in order to find peace.

What would ease the drug addict's pain when they're going through withdrawals? Their drug of choice. What will ease your anxiety and heartache when you're going through withdrawals? Your abuser.

However, this is only going to prolong your agony. You know you can't stay in a toxic relationship. Your abuser won't change, your situation will remain dire, and you'll be chasing your tail in the cycle of abuse again. Enduring this anxiety-riddled period will allow you to emotionally break away from your abuser.

You may have children with your abuser or financial ties. The same still applies: physically separate yourself from your abuser.

You may feel like it's impossible, but it's not. It takes extra planning, some tough self-talk, and the unequivocal understanding that you don't deserve the abuse you're enduring. Let me offer some tips and guidance in leading up to leaving. Before I go over this part, if you find yourself unable to plan and need to leave your situation quickly for fear of your safety, then follow your instincts. You can think about the practicalities later - for now, think about getting out, restraining orders and seeing what legal help is available to you.

Leading up to leaving doesn't mean you have a set date in mind (although perhaps you do have one), it just means you're preparing yourself as best you can for the inevitable. Practically speaking, you'll need these resources to leave:

Money

Important documentation such as passports and birth certificates

Bills and documents that prove your residence

Any evidence of the abuse compiled

Money, as well as the deep attachment you have with your abuser, may be a big factor in you staying in the relationship. To be more specific, the lack of money keeps you in the partnership. Ideally, you'd have a few months' living expenses saved up in order to leave, but I understand this isn't always viable, especially if your partner insists every penny is accounted for.

You need to be resourceful during this period of saving. If you can stash away money here and there in a separate (secret) bank account, that's great. If you'd struggle to do this, you need to get imaginative. If you had to raise £1,000, or more, within the next month or your life was at stake, would you manage to do it? I think most of us would. You'd do whatever it took. For me, I made a little pot of money by selling personal items my ex wouldn't have noticed had gone missing. I also took out a small loan at an exorbitant interest rate, although I don't recommend this unless it is a last resort.

Other people I've talked to who were in abusive relationships also hustled their way to a stash of money. Some made extra money online, some took extra shifts where they could, one even started up her own business selling homemade items to make more money. She under-egged her income from this to her abuser, allowing her to keep a portion of that revenue for herself.

You'll be amazed how resourceful we are when we need to be. Also, while it's natural that you fear surviving while finances seem like they're suffocating you, you'll be surprised at just how capable you are at getting by when you resolve to do so.

Important documentation is something you will benefit from taking with you when you leave. It can be hard to obtain if these things are being kept from you, but if you can hide them somewhere where you know you can grab them quickly, you'll have one less thing to worry about when leaving. You'll need your passport, drivers licence, bills, tax documents, proof of address, and credit or debit cards. Small sentimental items should be hidden to be picked up later, if possible; things like jewellery or photos.

A compilation of evidence of the abuse is also something you should heavily consider putting together, if you aren't already. This doesn't mean having a physical folder cataloguing your partner's cruelty towards you. This can be things like text messages, emails, bank statements that show all your money being transferred to them, images you've taken of injuries or damage to your property. Whatever your evidence is, you can collate it and store it safely, then delete it from your device. For me, I had a secret, separate email address that I forwarded all my evidence to. Images, documents, and screenshots that I knew would prove my partner's guilt if I ever needed to were sent to this covert email address.

I never logged into this email address on my phone, and anything I forwarded to this email address was swiftly deleted from my sent box. I was safe in the knowledge that everything I'd need was stored in my private inbox. I would periodically check this email address from my work computer, just to keep an eye on the rapidly building collection of documents in there. It also served as a sobering reminder as to just how poorly I was treated and served as a reality check to the severity of the abuse I was enduring. If you don't have access to another device that your partner can't access, I'd recommend taking a trip to your local library or business centre where use of a computer is often free (or relatively cheap to use). If you can't do this, an inexpensive flash drive can be used, if you take care to hide it well. Take advantage of the resources out there to create your own safe space to collate evidence and take those steps to secure your future self's peace of mind.

Take care of these seemingly small practicalities and you'll find you have less to fog your brain when you leave your abuser. Ideally, when you decide it's time to leave, you'll have your escape plan set in place. You'll know where you're going, be it a friend's house, a rented property, a shelter, or a family member's home, and you'll be prepared for the reaction of your abuser. This is key when leaving - protecting yourself. You know your abuser and you know how their warped need for retribution works. While this has kept you in their clutches up until this point, you have to fight this fear and use this knowledge to your advantage now.

The intricacies of leaving an abusive relationship differ from situation to situation. There is no clear cut blueprint, no one size fits all action plan, or book that can outline exactly what you need to do. You must leave, and do it as well prepared as you can. The next stage, however, does have a distinct set of actions, behaviours, and thought patterns you need to abide by to make sure that you detach yourself for good. It's called no contact. In order to maintain no contact with your abuser, you need to emotionally sever the ties you have, which helps you refrain from reaching out to them.

Emotionally breaking the bond and maintaining no contact

You don't need me to tell you that detaching yourself emotionally from your relationship is a task that seems unfeasible. Perhaps you don't really want to feel detached, either; that would mean feeling indifferent to your partner, and that's something you can't imagine ever happening. Me telling you that it's entirely possible to get to the stage of indifference might make you wince, but you need to understand that if you don't make this your primary goal, your health, sanity, and your future happiness is at stake. Separating yourself physically is undoubtedly the first step towards cutting the emotional ties that tether you to your partner. The rest is all a mental battle with yourself.

Your entire attitude and instinctive actions need to change. By detaching, which I'll go on to describe in more detail, not only are you putting a barrier in the way of you continuously being hurt, you're disarming the very person who keeps hurting you. How do they keep abusing you yet keep your unwavering love and loyalty? Because you are so emotionally attached to them, your abuser knows you won't leave. By working on detaching yourself from your abuser, they have no ammo to fire: they can't hurt you anymore. Sure, they can still name-call, tell lies about you, or try and tarnish your name. But you can get yourself to a point where that shouldn't matter - because, in reality, it doesn't. Your health and wellbeing does. If your spouse (ex-spouse at this point) wants to place all of their energy, effort, and thought into bringing you down, that's their choice. It's not because they miss you or are unable to cope without you, they're acting out because their subservient victim has found their self-worth.

To battle through this period, you need to maintain your stance, and focus on reaching the point of indifference and no emotional attachment. To help you detach, let me try and make some points that are logical and based on fact - things an abusive partner tends not to offer up.

First of all, and this is going to be hard to hear, your spouse doesn't love you. It's like a punch in the gut to comprehend, but once you accept this - or rather, stop accepting a toxic imitation of love - then you can begin tearing yourself away from the twisted person you're attached to.

Secondly, the ability to strip the power away from your abuser is in your hands. Of course, when you're in the midst of an abusive episode or being gaslighted and lied to left right and centre, this seems like a stupid, outlandish thought. But once you start making an effort to clear the fog in your mind and view your relationship with clarity and logic, you'll understand you have much more power than you think. Your abuser's self-worth and feelings of superiority and dominance are all tied up in their ability to abuse and manipulate you. If you take that away, you pull the rug from underneath them. You hold that power.

A third point I'd like to make is that you do not 'need' your abuser. You might have feelings like you'll never meet anyone else or have anyone else want you. Money and housing problems might make you think you're unable to survive without your abuser. Your health or family commitments may make you doubt your ability to get by without your spouse.

Whatever reason or reasons you have that make you think you 'need' your abuser are thoughts you've had drilled into you by your partner, either directly by their words or indirectly through their actions. The same goes for you feeling like you'll die if you can't be with your partner. Yes, the separation hurts, but the pain doesn't last. Nobody ever died of a broken heart. Shattered hearts can always be mended, time and an abundance of self-care takes care of that.

My fourth point is to remind you that you're not responsible for your partner's happiness. The thought of them coping without you might fill you with panic and worry. The things they'll do without you around might make you feel sick to your stomach, but this isn't your burden to bear. Their shortcomings and inadequacies aren't your issues to address or be concerned with.

I'd like you to keep this fifth point especially at the forefront of your mind: if you persist in holding out hope for your partner to change or for the relationship to improve, you are building yourself up for even greater pain. You are disillusioning your reality to try and alleviate some of the pain you're going through, I understand that. But please remember the abuse you're going through won't ever stop. Sure, there may be lulls and periods of happiness, but it'll never stop. The cycle doesn't stop: you have to get out.

At the risk of sounding like a broken record, I'd also like to remind you that you are not helpless. You are responsible for you, just as your abuser is responsible for themselves. Your well-being depends on you, and walking away from a destructive, toxic relationship is non-negotiable when it comes to safeguarding your health and sanity. Please remember to cast aside feelings that keep you trapped in the relationship. Shame, incompetency, and fear have all been instilled into you to keep you locked in the cycle of abuse and in the clutches of your abuser.

These feelings don't serve you. They don't keep you safe, don't protect your mental health, don't feed your self-worth. When you begin to feel the twinges of, 'What will people think?' or, 'I'm ashamed of leaving the relationship with nothing,' you need to mentally put them in a box and tape it tightly. There is zero shame in leaving something that damages you, and acknowledging as much isn't something you should shy away from.

Now that I've covered the points I'd like you to keep in mind, let me go over some detachment techniques. Ideally, you will practise these while you're physically apart from your abuser when you've left them, and utilise them to reach indifference. You can still practise these mental techniques while in the relationship to help you make the leap to freedom, but they do work best while the abuser is out of sight. Getting them out of mind is stage two.

Detachment Technique #1:

Understand and destroy the emotional hooks your abuser has over you.

An emotional hook is something your abuser holds over your head, a stake you have in the relationship. Of course, they'll hover this over you and use this emotional hook to their advantage. An example of this could be your abuser using guilt so you don't wriggle off that hook. 'I can't take care of myself without you,' or 'How do you expect the kids to get fed if you left?' are both guilt-trips to tighten the grip the abuser has over you.

Another emotional hook that can be used against you is loss. 'You know I can meet someone else better than you,' or 'I have so much to offer and someone else will appreciate that,' are phrases used to make you feel like you'd suffer a devastating loss should you leave the relationship. 'You'll never meet anyone like me again,' is another, often-used quote by egotistical abusers wanting to hook their victim back in with the fear of them losing something good. Loss of status or material possessions are also frequently used as emotional hooks.

Think about what your emotional hooks are. What triggers you into a state of fear or panic or dread, causing you to remain in the partnership? Your abuser knows exactly what these are and uses them to their advantage. You need to identify them and work on demolishing them. Write them down and think about why these things trigger you so much. Do you fear never meeting someone else? Are you afraid of your partner meeting someone else and replacing you? Are you worried that you'll lose your place in the community or be exiled? Whatever you feel, consider why you feel this way. Think about the worst-case scenario - your fear comes true. If it does, why is it worth sacrificing your health and happiness to ensure it doesn't happen? Why are you abandoning yourself out of fear of these threats becoming reality?

Detachment Technique #2:

Remember the suffering you've endured.

A bit of a bleak thing to ask you to do, especially when the point of this book is to help you break the cycle of suffering, but hear me out. I don't mean for you to sit and ruminate on every vile and despicable thing your partner has done to you, but rather, don't downplay or edit just how bad things were in the relationship. After all, you've done this in the past and given your abuser the benefit of the doubt that things would change, only to be smacked in the face with the same abhorrent behaviour over and over again. To be perpetually in a state of heartache and disappointment isn't something you want to be, so use your past suffering to build up the courage and self-worth to create boundaries. If you don't? Then you can expect more of the same. After all, the best predictor for future behaviour is past behaviour.

Remember, your expectations of your partner have been low. You wanted to be treated humanely, to be respected, to be loved. These are very basic components of a healthy relationship, and you were withheld these basic rights frequently. In the beginning, you were lured in with these things, but once you were caught in the trap, that facade was dropped. Still, you stayed with your abuser hoping and wishing and even sometimes believing things would change for the better.

Breaking the trauma bond is all about switching your thought patterns. Facing the harsh reality of what you've been through will accelerate you on your path to healing tenfold. Remember the bigger picture. It's so easy to be weighed down by your current situation, which makes returning to your abuser feel like the easiest thing to do. But, your aim is to get to a point where your abuser no longer has the power to affect you, and remembering the extreme horror you've endured at their hands can serve to build an emotional barrier between you and them.

Detachment Technique #3:

Centre yourself.

This is a trick I learned while I was still with my abuser, but I found it worked even better for me when I got out of the relationship. When you feel overwhelmed, stressed, full of anxiety and worry, centering yourself can help you balance your emotions. In times like this, when your emotions are incredibly heightened, rebalancing yourself can help you think more logically and rationally.

First, you need to locate your centre of gravity, which is the physical balance point of your body. In females, this is just below the belly button. For males, it's just above the belly button. Take a moment now to locate it, both physically and mentally. Place your hand there while focusing on that area in your mind. It's called your 'balance point' because that's exactly what it is; it's where your lower and upper body weight is balanced. Miraculously, you can also use it to balance your emotions.

When negative emotions begin to swamp you, focus on your balance point. Take the time to remind yourself that you are in control. You are in the driving seat of your own life, and you choose how to navigate that. Affirm these facts while you take a deep breath in and out. Do this half a dozen times, or more if you need to, while focusing on your balance point.

When you begin to feel a bit calmer, then you can redirect that negative energy you've been retaining. All of that stress, anxiety, panic and worry you have flowing around your body, imagine it making its way to your balance point. Picture it however you like. Maybe you see the negative energy like flowing lava, or maybe you see it like a green poison that you're extracting from your body. How you choose to imagine this is up to you. I imagine my balance point has a pot collecting all of the toxic energy, and once it's full, I can empty it from my being. When I've felt particularly upset or panicked, I even imagine myself throwing the pot far, far away from myself where it explodes in mid air.

Now you've expelled the badness and toxic energy, it's time to focus on the good energy you want to invite into your life. Think about the things you want to achieve, and repeat them to yourself as you inhale and exhale.

'I will break free from the hold my abuser has over me'

'I am strong enough to be without my abuser and deserve better'

'I am a good person who deserves happiness'

'I am in control of my life'

Whatever you want your focus to be, keep repeating it.

While you will find it hard to want to do much during this period of emotional turmoil, it's important for your mental and physical health to do something that distracts you from thinking about your abuser. This could be immersing yourself in a hobby or activity you weren't able to do while in the relationship. Things like reading, going to the gym, drawing, creating things... Whatever your relationship prevented you from doing, make a point of doing it now.

This exercise helps immensely when you feel like reaching out to your abuser or checking their social media. Before you put yourself through that, centre yourself and you'll find the urge to reach out has been replaced by a reminder of just how cruelly you've been treated. This brings me to my next point: how you can refrain from reaching out to your abuser when you feel an overwhelming desire to do so.

Keeping no contact

First: block, block, block.

Email, phone numbers, social media accounts. I even changed bank accounts because my ex sent me money with abuse in the reference. Whatever avenue that you have open for your abuser to contact you, hit the block button. After you've blocked them, delete their number. Even though you might know it off by heart, the physical act of removing them from your phone or contact list is you taking back your power.

Should there be a reason you need to contact them, an intermediary is the best option. Ideally not anyone close to either them or you. For your own sanity and to ensure the best outcome for yourself, you need as much distance between you and your abuser as possible.

It's natural you'll wonder what your ex is doing, who they're with or how they're coping. When we can't speak to them or see them, we can make up all sorts of scenarios in our minds, leading us to breaking no contact by either reaching out to them or unblocking them on social media to see what they're up to. Do not do this. Put your phone away, close your laptop, and go for a walk. Get some fresh air. Remember what this person did to you.

Second to blocking your ex on every communication avenue possible is to remove any photos and messages you have from them on your devices. Remember to keep the incriminating and threatening messages stored in your safe place, but be sure to remove any messages or pictures that can cause you to look at the relationship with a falsified memory. Of course you had happy times throughout your time with your ex, it's part of the abuse cycle. To keep reminders of this will only serve to draw you back into that cycle. Remove them. It might hurt at first, and your finger may hover over the 'delete' button for a while before you go ahead and press. But, you need to commit to doing whatever it takes to maintain no contact.

Should your ex find a way to contact you, don't reply. Even replying, *do not contact me anymore, I don't want anything to do with you* is a big no-no. It lets your abuser know they have enough control over you to entice a response. This reinforces to them that they can still, with a little manipulation, reel you back in. Be it via scaring you, love bombing you, or guilt tripping you, by acknowledging an open method of communication, you're taking five steps back in your journey to peace and happiness. Even if they threaten to expose personal things about you or say they'll do something awful if you don't reply or return to the relationship, do not be manipulated by the abuser. Keep the texts in your dossier of evidence, and resist the urge to act upon the things your ex is saying.

People who know your ex may try to keep you in the loop about what they're doing or things they're saying about you. From experience, cutting these people off was the best thing I did for my mental health. Some of these individuals may be well-meaning, and if you believe this to be true, kindly ask them not to pass any updates about your ex to you. Also, request that they don't go back to your ex with any information about you. You may find, however, loyalties can be tested, and mutual friends may be giving your ex information about you that you really don't want them knowing, such as where you are and what you're doing. If this boundary is crossed, my advice is to put that friendship on hold and reassess if they're someone you'd want in your life moving forward.

There may be times when you think to yourself, why am I doing this? When you go through leaving an abuser and setting up the no contact boundary, you're also going through the grieving process. You're suffering the loss of the same person who gave you intermittent comfort and who you felt so unwaveringly attached to. You will trudge through the episodes of denial, the frustration and injustice, the outbursts of anger. You'll need to deal with the want to bargain with your ex, as well as the low periods of wondering why things couldn't be different. These emotions are part of the grieving process, something you have to go through in order to reach acceptance.

When you feel so heavy and lost without your abuser, the want to speak to them can feel uncontrollable. However, it's not. Remember, the only person who can control you is you. So, before you do the unthinkable and send that text or send a friend request, grab a piece of paper and headline it, **Why I Must Not Contact My Abuser**. Fill the page. Write all of the reasons you left the relationship and why you must stay the course. It could be things like:

My ex treated me like an emotional punch bag.

My ex lied to me and made me believe I was the toxic one.

My ex made me feel like I was crazy.

My ex got me into debt.

My ex refuses to see their wrongdoing.

My ex is violent and possessive.

Write it all down and once you've purged those bad memories onto the page, take a step back and read it. Why would you put yourself through all of this again? The hope you've always held out for your partner to change has never materialised, and it won't materialise should you reach out to them. As heavy as it feels, you need to adhere to the boundaries you've put in place. The urge to contact them does fade away, although I know that when you're itching to speak to them it doesn't feel that way.

Self-compassion during the aftermath of abuse

It may feel like you're far, far away from this point right now. If you're reading this book, there likely is no 'aftermath' just yet - you're still in the trenches, tied to your abuser. Despite almost every fibre of your being trying to tell you otherwise, let me tell you that dealing with the aftermath of abuse is nowhere near as painful as enduring it indefinitely. Still, it's an emotionally strenuous time, one that often gets overlooked. People often speak of getting out of an abusive situation, but what about afterwards?

Things like the urge to reach out and run back to the relationship fizzle out surprisingly quickly once you're away from your abuser. Not necessarily weeks after you've left, but much quicker than you'd imagine. The days you spend thinking about them or what they're up to turn into hours which evaporate into minutes until eventually, you have entire days pass where you don't think about your ex. And, even then, you may spend a few moments pondering your past life, but you find you snap back into the present without much effort. The pining for your ex really doesn't consume you for as long as you think it will, but there are other aftereffects that do last longer and need your attention.

When you left the relationship, as well as the trauma and emotional baggage you need to unpack, you left with a skewed sense of self. Let me cover them so you're aware of the seemingly small things you're enduring (that turn into bigger things if you don't address them). Feelings of guilt, blame, and not being good enough plague you, even if you don't fully realise it. To stop these toxic feelings in their tracks, you need to be mindful of your self-talk and avoid becoming a self-fulfilling prophecy.

This period of your life, more than any other period you're likely to go through, needs you to fully engage in self-compassion. Not self-pity, bear in mind - that just feeds the negative feelings you're already contending with. Self-compassion is a nurturing way of treating yourself, not a woe-is-me way. If you succumb to being self-critical, you become your abuser as well as a victim of yourself.

For so long, you've been used to put-downs and criticism. It's almost so familiar it's a comfort. From being berated and treated poorly by our partner, this eventually trickled into our own psyche, and changed the way we speak to ourselves. Self-criticism rears its head when our threat-defence system is triggered. It's how our partner conditioned us to be, and it's a tough habit to break even when they're out of the picture.

As I mentioned earlier, a symptom of a toxic relationship is hypervigilance, which sees us feeling threatened even in situations where there is no danger. This overwhelming feeling of threat can trigger self-critique, which ought to be swiftly swapped with self-compassion. When we swap the two methods, we learn to turn off the threat-defence response and replace it with a compassionate one. This is important, because the threat response only gives us negative outcomes. You'll have heard of the *fight, flight, freeze* reactions, and that's exactly what perceived threat offers us as responses. Fight means we fight ourselves with cruel self-talk, flight means we avoid interaction and isolate ourselves to avoid further threat, and freeze sees us stopping to overthink our situation.

To combat these negative responses, we need to mindfully practice compassion towards ourselves. We need security and safety, not uncertainty and fear. Not only do you owe yourself that, you can offer yourself that. To start your journey towards self-compassion, you need to cut off anything or anyone who will put you in harm's way, and understand that saying no doesn't make you a bad person. You need to put yourself first and not feel beholden to others' expectations of you, particularly while you're going through the heavy struggle of leaving a bad relationship.

Protecting yourself means saying no to others who are hurting us or to the harm we inflict on ourselves, often in unconscious ways. 'No' can be a full sentence without a follow-up explanation or reasoning. We owe it to ourselves to self-soothe when we need to, instead of berating ourselves. We need to understand that we are worthy of good things, and doing things to manifest that isn't selfishness, it's providing yourself with what you deserve.

You don't need me to tell you that life can be hard. Why do you want to make it even more difficult by being hard on yourself?

Imagine self-compassion as being your internal friend. Just as a friend in real life could sit you down, listen to your worries and concerns, and offer you comfort and a plan of action to overcome them, you can offer that same compassion to yourself. Don't be resistant to this way of thinking because you believe it to be self-indulgent or self-pampering. Open yourself up to receiving the concern, warmth, and understanding you've been deprived of for so long. Check in with yourself throughout the day and ask yourself two important questions: 'How am I feeling?' 'What do I need?' You might not have the answer right away, but connecting to yourself in this way helps you navigate your way towards a solution.

The next step to a healthier way of thinking is to leave perfection, or your idea of perfection, at the door. Imperfection is life, and none of us are flawless creatures in any aspect. It's what makes us human, and you need to remember this before you succumb to negative-self talk.

During this emotionally tumultuous time, it's also a good idea to create a strong, reliable support system for yourself. This may feel tricky or unattainable if you've cut off friends and family, but you'll surprise yourself at how many people would love for you to reach out to them. Sure, some people may be less understanding, but that's their decision to make. Focus on the good things you can invite into your life. If you can schedule some time for hobbies or take a class doing something you're interested in, you can begin forming new relationships with brand new people, something that can really help pull you from dark periods of your life. As closed off as you may feel to doing this, I can't stress just how freeing and re-energising it is to do the things you were afraid to do during the relationship.

Don't close yourself off to the world. It might not feel like it right now, but there's a lot of good people out there.

Moving Forward

Thank you for reading Stockholm Syndrome in a Relationship: Breaking The Toxic Cycle of Trauma Bonding. I hope this book has gone some way into helping you understand your trauma bond or has given you the empowerment you need to eventually sever the ties and break the cycle of abuse.

Stockholm syndrome in a relationship is still, in my opinion, not understood by many, including those who are engulfed in the trauma trap. I hope this book has helped you understand more about this complex type of abuse and how it escalates so rapidly and has a grip so tight that escaping seems unfathomable. But, I also hope it can show you that breaking the chains is possible, that you can survive (and thrive) without your abuser. It takes some adjustment of your thinking, building up your mental strength, and an abundance of willpower, but it's within reach.

Remember, the only thing you can control is you.

FIND ME AT LIVJESSON.com or search for my name on all socials: @LivJesson. I look forward to connecting with you!

About the Author

Liv is a writer, wine drinker, and a big lover of nature and animals.

She writes primarily about the traumas of toxic relationships and how to overcome them, citing her own experiences along the way.

Read more at livjesson.com.

www.ingramcontent.com/pod-product-compliance
Lightning Source LLC
Chambersburg PA
CBHW071346130726
47996CB00002B/832